THE FIRST BOOK OF
THE EARLY SETTLERS

In the early 1600's several companies went to the New World

THE FIRST BOOK OF
THE EARLY SETTLERS

by LOUISE DICKINSON RICH

Pictures by
DOUGLAS GORSLINE

FRANKLIN WATTS, INC.
845 Third Avenue, New York, N.Y. 10022

The Library of Congress has catalogued this book as follows:

Rich, Louise (Dickinson) 1903–
    The first book of early settlers. Pictures by Douglas Gorsline.
New York, F. Watts 1959

    85 p.   illus.   23 cm. (First book series 96)

        1. U. S.—Soc. life & cust.—Colonial period.   2. U. S.—History, Juvenile.
I. Title

E162.R5   973.2   59–5255 ‡

Library of Congress

CONTENTS

Sighting the new land

1

EVEN BEFORE THE SETTLERS —

The first English settlers of eastern North America did not come to a land that was entirely unknown. Even before Columbus, the Vikings had sailed along the coast of what are now New England and Nova Scotia; and after Columbus, all through the 1500's, fishing fleets from England and France had commonly made two or three trips a year to the waters of the New World to fill their holds with cod, herring, and pollack. The New World fisheries were an important source of food for European countries.

In the course of these voyages the crews often landed to stretch their legs, pick berries, fill their water casks, wash clothes, repair their gear, and dry their catches in the sun. Thus they became acquainted at least with the land along the coast; but since their interest was chiefly in catching fish and getting home as soon as possible, they never made more than temporary camps on shore.

Other groups from European countries came simply to explore. Most of them were looking either for treasures of gold and gems, or for a passage to India. At that time the wealth of the world in silks, jewels, and spices lay in the Orient, and people thought it important to find a short and easy route from Europe to the East. The country that controlled such a route would have a great advantage over the other countries. In seeking this passage, explorers learned various things about North America. And they brought home various opinions, among them the idea that Europeans could never live in any part of the country north of the Hudson River's mouth, as the climate was too harsh.

So you see, it was common knowledge that over the western horizon lay a great continent, although no one realized how great. Nor did anyone know what that continent held in the way of riches and resources, dangers and disadvantages. There was gossip of wealth in the form of furs, lumber, and gold; but there was also fear of hostile Indians, the bitter cold of the North, and the damp heat of the South. However, the same idea finally came to a large number of people: it would be possible actually to live in the New World.

But people do not pack up and move to a strange, uninhabited, and forbidding land thousands of miles away without a good reason. Moving thus is too dangerous and uncertain. It is not easy to leave a familiar home when making a new one is bound to be difficult.

Nevertheless, in the early 1600's several companies did leave their homes and did go to the New World to settle. Each group had its own reasons for leaving, although the reasons were not the same for all. However, once it arrived, each company was faced with the same problem: that of making a home and supporting itself in a wilderness, in unknown surroundings and an unfamiliar climate, and among Indians who might possibly turn out to be enemies. Each company dealt with the problem in its own way. Some of the very earliest companies failed, but several colonies between Virginia and Massachusetts were finally established. They were not at all alike, in spite of the fact that they all started out with much the same material to work on.

Their differences depended chiefly on three things: what the people who made up each separate company were like; why each went to the New World; and how each went about the business of living there.

In 1607 three ships dropped anchor at Jamestown

2

THE JAMESTOWN VENTURERS

On May 13, 1607, three ships dropped anchor about thirty miles above the mouth of the James River in Virginia. They were the *Susan Constant,* the *Discovery,* and the *Goodspeed,* owned by the Virginia Company of London and under the command of Captain Christopher Newport. Aboard them were one hundred and five men known as the Virginia Venturers. They had been sent out by the Company under what was really a business agreement. The Virginia Company was giving them an opportunity in the New World and supporting them while they were settling their colony. For their part, the Venturers were to look for a Northwest Passage to the Orient and to repay the Company in whatever products the country might have; the directors mentioned mineral ores particularly. Since they had very little idea of what Virginia was like, the directors gave strict orders that no one should send back to England any stories of hardship. Members of the Company did not wish to discourage possible future settlers.

The Venturers were a rather mixed group. Over half of them were listed as "gentlemen," who never in their lives had worked with their hands. Most of these men had signed up in search of excitement and adventure. Among the other settlers were a tailor, a jeweler, and even a perfumer. Only a few were the workers who were so badly needed — carpenters, farmers, bricklayers, and stonemasons. These few came to Virginia in hopes of bettering themselves, since there was little opportunity for workingmen in England.

One man stood out from the beginning: Captain John Smith, an explorer. Very soon, although he was not officially in command, the others found themselves looking to him for leadership. Many disliked him, as he was somewhat bossy, but almost everybody listened to his advice and obeyed his orders.

It was spring when the Venturers arrived, and as they sailed up the river the country was beautiful. One of the company, George Percy, wrote of it in this way: "This river which we have discovered is one of the famousest rivers that ever was found by any Christian. It ebbs and flows a hundred and three-score miles, where ships of great burden may harbor in safety. Wheresoever we landed upon this river, we saw the goodliest woods as beech, oak, cedar, cypress, walnuts, sassafras, and vines in great abundance, which hang in great clusters on many trees, and other trees unknown; and all the grounds are spread with many sweet and delicate flowers of diverse colors and kinds. There are also many fruits as strawberries, mulberries,

The landing party fired their muskets to frighten the Indians

raspberries, and fruits unknown. There are many branches of this river, which run flowing through the woods with great plenty of fish of all kinds. . . . There is also great store of deer both red and fallow. There are bears, foxes, otters, beavers, muskrats, and wild beasts unknown."

The expedition chose a small peninsula jutting into the river for the site of their colony, which they named Jamestown in honor of the king. This was not the best location, as the land was low, swampy, and unhealthful; but there was good anchorage for the ships and it was a position easy to defend. Earlier a landing party had been attacked by Indians, whom they had frightened away with the noise of their unfamiliar muskets.

Now, first of all, the party set to work building a triangular

Sawing logs for the stockade

fort, with cannon mounted at each angle and with the dwelling places within it. This fort was simply a high stockade of rough logs set in the ground and fastened together with vines. Even so, it was not easy to build. There were only a few carpenters in the whole group. To each of these men a crew of "gentlemen," or Cavaliers, was assigned. The carpenters were to teach their crews to use axes and saws. These men felled the trees and, after trimming off the branches, sawed them into logs. Other groups were chosen to mow grass and bind it into bundles of thatch for roofing, to make fishing nets, and to dig gardens.

The Cavaliers were not used to labor, and some of them had a hard time. Their hands blistered and their muscles became lame and sore. Soon the air was blue with curses. In his history of Jamestown, John Smith tells how later he dealt with this situation. He asked the foreman of each gang to keep account of the oaths, and for every one a man used during the day, a can of cold water was poured down his sleeve that night. The swearing stopped almost at once.

The workingmen had proper clothes for their labor. They wore full knee breeches called "slops," made out of wool or a mixture of linen and wool called linsey-woolsey; linen shirts; and leather or wool jackets, or jerkins. On their feet were sturdy shoes, and on their heads comfortable knit caps. John Smith and the few soldiers wore steel breastplates and helmets, which would be useless against modern bullets but would easily turn an arrow. But in addition to their other troubles the gentlemen had to work in most unsuitable clothes. They were dressed for London society in graceful, wide-brimmed hats with curling plumes; ruffled silk shirts; sweeping cloaks; and soft, high boots with wide tops. They must have felt both ridiculous and uncomfortable; and yet one of the accounts written at the time speaks especially of how "pleasantly" most of them took on each unfamiliar task. They made an adventure and a joke out of everything.

For all their work, the new little settlement was not very impressive. The weather was warm, and the colonists decided not to build houses for a while. Instead, they put up tents or crude huts which had thatched roofs held up on forked posts. The walls were made by driving poles into the ground a few

9

inches apart and weaving willow branches and vines in and out between them, then daubing the whole with mud. There were no chimneys — just a hole in the roof to let out the smoke. Usually the settlers cooked in the open anyhow.

In place of a church, a board was nailed between two trees for a reading desk, and a canvas was stretched over it for shelter. Here the Rev. Robert Hunt conducted daily Church of England services and gave two sermons every Sunday.

The settlers did not bother to dig a well, but drank the water from the river. Food was a much more serious problem than shelter. The voyage had taken much longer than planned — over five months — and the food supply the settlers had brought was almost exhausted. There were oysters and fish in the river and plenty of game in the woods, but the settlers with their loud guns and heavy boots were noisy hunters, and poor shots as well. The native wild rice, berries, and yams were not yet ripe. Something had to be done at once.

Captain Newport decided to explore the country further and at the same time to try to get help from the Indians. He picked a group of twenty-two men to go with him, among them John Smith. Then he set the others to making clapboards and digging sassafras roots to send back to England in the ships. The Virginia Company would expect some return on their investment, and there was a great demand for lumber in England.

The explorers set off up the James River valley. The Indians whom they met along the way seemed friendly, although they

The Indians were friendly, but had no corn to trade

had no corn to trade. They depended on corn for their food and had only enough to last until the fall crop was ripe. They thought the Englishmen had come to America simply as visitors and they made them welcome. The explorers let them think they were staying only a short time; it seemed the easiest way to keep peace. But when they returned to the fort, they found that two hundred warriors, probably suspecting their real plans, had attacked Jamestown and had killed one man and wounded several. This was the beginning of trouble with the Indians that continued off and on for many years.

In June, Newport sailed for England with his clapboards and

sassafras. He left behind all the food he could spare, but this wasn't much. There were a few hens and a tiny supply of wheat and barley — just enough so that each man could have a pint a day. They boiled the grain and ate this gruel, and they drank the river water.

The weather grew hotter and hotter, and this bothered the colonists, who were not used to heat. The river shrank between its banks and grew muddy and slimy. The heat, the foul water, and the hard work brought on a wave of sickness — malaria, cholera, dysentery, and typhoid fever — so that many of the settlers died. Finally only thirty-eight remained of the original one hundred and five. Even these men were in a pitiful condition, barely able to drag themselves around when autumn came.

Things improved a little then. The weather cooled and large flocks of migrating wildfowl covered the river and swamps, so that the settlers were able to shoot hundreds of them. Although the colony itself had raised no corn, Smith was able to trade beads, knives, and trinkets for small amounts of it. He knew this supply would not last the winter, however, so he decided to go up the Chickahominy River to see what he could collect from the tribes there.

As the party was wading through White Oak Swamp, a band of Indians attacked it, killing Smith's companions and taking him prisoner. They marched him to the longhouse of Powhatan, the very powerful chief of all the tribes in the area. Powhatan was beginning to feel sure that the English had no idea of going

Pocahontas asked that Powhatan spare Smith's life

home, but intended to stay and take over his hunting grounds. He was far from friendly. In fact, as John Smith told the story years later, he ordered Smith to be clubbed to death.

Smith went on to say that Powhatan's young daughter Pocahontas, impressed by his blond good looks, risked her life by

13

flinging herself between him and the clubs. This is probably not entirely true. Among the North American Indian tribes there was a custom that the life of any captive should be spared at the request of a tribe member. Usually the rescued victim was then adopted by the tribe, and often lived with them thereafter. So it is very likely that Pocahontas did not risk her life at all, but simply asked her father to spare Smith. Following custom, Powhatan did so.

In any case, Smith was now on friendly terms with the Indians, and fortunately so. At this time of very great need the natives came to the village with supplies of corn and game. Without that help the settlers surely would have perished.

At about the time that Smith returned home from his narrow escape, Captain Newport arrived in Jamestown with what became known as the "First Supply" of new settlers and provisions. There were one hundred and twenty men. This brought the number in the colony up to one hundred and fifty-eight, but there was not enough food to feed even the survivors of that summer. So Smith went back to Powhatan, taking with him Captain Newport and a good supply of trading goods.

Smith let Newport do the talking, and Newport was not a good trader. He was too straightforward and honest. He spread out all the goods he had and asked how much corn Powhatan would give for them. Powhatan would go no higher than four bushels, which would not last even a day among so many colonists. But by accident some blue beads had been held out, chiefly because they were too few and cheap to bother with. Smith, who was a very shrewd trader, showed them to the chief and explained that they were very precious; only royalty was allowed to wear beads like these; he couldn't possibly let Powhatan have them at any price.

Naturally, Powhatan felt he *had* to have them. Finally Smith — doubtless making it seem like a big favor — let them go for over two hundred bushels of corn. After that, Newport allowed him to do the bargaining with the natives; but the damage was done. From then on, Powhatan continually complained that Smith was mean and grasping, since he expected so much more for his money than Newport had. It became very hard to deal with the chief, who distrusted the settlers anyhow. And you really can't blame him for that.

With the new supplies and the new settlers, Jamestown should have been able to get onto its feet before Captain Newport returned again to England. All that was needed was a little honest effort. But a very unfortunate thing happened. The Company in London had always expressed its interest in minerals, and on his first voyage Newport had taken back a sample of what appeared to be gold. Now again, apparently, the Company had emphasized its interest in minerals, especially gold. At about this time someone stumbled onto what were thought to be traces of this mineral.

The Spanish explorers had found gold in Mexico; why not the English in Virginia? Jamestown went gold-crazy. No one

The village at Jamestown burned

really cared to work dully at building homes for the newcomers, preparing for future crops of corn, or making clapboards to send back to the Company. Gold-hunting was much more exciting. Even when the whole village burned flat and rats ate what corn there was, the colonists were not interested in repairing the damage. Finally, however, Newport sailed for England — but without a cargo of gold.

Within the next few months the Second and Third Supplies of too many persons and too little food arrived. The new colonists had entirely the wrong idea of what to expect and what was expected of them. Because no bad news had been allowed to get back to England, they pictured Virginia as a sort of paradise. They soon discovered that here everyone worked for the community. If a man shot a deer, raised a bushel of corn, or split a cord of clapboards, it was not his. It was shared by everyone. What, then, they thought, was the point of working? Let someone more foolish do so. Finally thirty or forty men were supporting the whole colony of several hundred. Smith had to put his foot down. He announced that anybody who did not work, did not eat; and he meant it.

Then, in the fall of 1609, Smith was badly burned in a gunpowder explosion and had to go back to England. The settlers continued their shiftless way of life, without a good leader, and suddenly discovered that they did not have anything to eat. As the days grew shorter and colder, food became more and more scarce. They ate acorns, nuts, roots, fruits, whatever they could find. Then they ate the dogs. Then they caught frogs and snakes and toads and ate them.

It was what has become known as the "Starving Time," and starve they really did. Jamestown became a settlement of walking skeletons and scarecrows, of bundles of skin and bones and rags, hardly able to crawl in and out of their miserable hovels. When Smith left, there had been over five hundred people in the colony. By spring only about sixty of them were alive.

These few survivors decided that they had best give up and go home. They loaded aboard their small boats and set off downriver, hoping to find some means of shipping overseas when they came to the coast. They had not gone very far, however, when they saw a sail. The Company had sent out another expedition under Lord De la Warr to bring supplies and aid to Jamestown. The colonists turned around and went back, and Jamestown was saved.

Up until this time the colony had spent most of its energies simply in staying alive. Even so, some of the settlers had tried off and on to make money for the Company by more practical means than searching for gold. There had been the clapboards and sassafras root. A little later a group of glass blowers had set up a glass-making business. Others tried to manufacture tar and soap, to smelt iron, or to raise grapes for wine. None of these enterprises was very successful. Once in a while, too, someone collected a little of the coarse native tobacco that the Indians smoked, and shipped it to England; but it was too harsh and strong for the Europeans. Now a newcomer named John Rolfe began thinking seriously about tobacco.

He was interested in experimenting with plants. Why not see what could be done with tobacco? He obtained seeds from the West Indies and South America. Working patiently with these, he found new and better ways of growing and curing the tobacco leaf so that it was acceptable in Europe. This took time, but at long last his experiments resulted in tobacco's becoming the true wealth and support of the colony.

But John Rolfe contributed more than that. For very good reasons Powhatan had never really liked the English and as time went on his tribes became more troublesome. One of the

John Rolfe was attracted to Pocahontas

men in charge at Jamestown, Samuel Argall, decided that the
best way to control the chief would be to kidnap Pocahontas
and hold her as a hostage. This he succeeded in doing.

When she came to the colony, Rolfe was deeply attracted to
her and she to him. She seems to have been a really beautiful,
brave, and intelligent girl who knew her own mind. She begged
her father to allow her to marry Rolfe, and the old chief finally
agreed. Pocahontas and John Rolfe were married in the Jamestown church, with Pocahontas' uncle and two of her brothers
present in all their feathers and paint.

This marriage put an end to Indian trouble for some time to
come, since Powhatan felt he should help his new in-laws rather

than hinder them. The marriage came just in time, too. In order to raise tobacco and other crops successfully, the colonists had to leave the protection of the fort and live on widely scattered plantations, where they would have more room. They never could have done this if the Indians had been hostile; but now the forest was cleared in all directions, and Jamestown began to prosper, mainly through tobacco, but with the help of other products.

And so, after many years of hardship and at the cost of many lives and much money, the first permanent English colony in the New World was established. There had been no Northwest Passage to India, no rich gold mines, no wonderful treasure of gems. All there had been was a common weed growing right under the settlers' noses. But as it turned out, that was enough.

3

THE PLYMOUTH PILGRIMS

Francis Billington was eight years old when the Pilgrims landed at Plymouth in December, 1620, and his brother Johnny was six. All those aboard the *Mayflower* were glad to end the voyage of over two months across the rough autumn sea, but the two boys were perhaps happiest of all. Every one of the hundred-and-two passengers had suffered from the steady diet of hardtack and "salt horse" — corned beef or pork — and from being continually cold, wet, and seasick. The girls and women also complained of never being able to bathe or change into clean clothes, but this did not bother the boys very much.

What they minded most was the cramped quarters and lack of space to romp and run with the only animals aboard: a mastiff, a spaniel, and the ship's cats. Every inch of room was crammed with all the things necessary for the trip and for making new homes in a land where there were no shops and no neighbors: clothes and tools and blankets; cooking utensils,

John Alden inspected the water barrels every day

fishing equipment and coils of rope; kegs of powder and shot; and the great casks of water that the cooper, John Alden, inspected every day for leaks.

Sometimes he let Francis and Johnny help him, explaining how serious it would be to run out of drinking water in mid-ocean. And sometimes Captain Myles Standish told them stories of his travels. Captain Standish was not a Separatist as some of the other Pilgrims were. He had been hired as a military leader, since the Pilgrims knew nothing about warfare and they might have to fight the Indians. But neither was the boys' father a Separatist. His family was one of a group that had joined the expedition to make up the proper number of settlers.

The boys were not much interested in why the others had

chosen to leave England for a wilderness land, but they couldn't help learning that some of the Pilgrims had separated from the Church of England. This was against the law and a dangerous thing to do. Separatists could be punished by death. However, this group, led by John Carver, William Bradford, and William Brewster, disapproved so strongly of the candles, incense, prayer books, and ceremony of the official church that they were willing to risk their lives. They believed that a church service should be very simple, with only Bible readings, prayers not taken from a prayer book, and a sermon by the minister. This was how they intended to worship in North Virginia, as New England was then sometimes called. That was why they left England.

All this the boys found tiresome. Few forests in England were open to the public at this time, and they looked forward to a new country to explore, woods to roam in, and perhaps adventures with Indians. When land was sighted on November 19, 1620, they could hardly contain themselves. The landfall proved to be the end of Cape Cod — what is now Province-town. Still nobody was allowed ashore. The leaders decided that first a form of government should be established, and they drew up a paper called the Mayflower Compact. This was signed by almost every man aboard and bound them to obey the officers they would elect and the laws they would pass. Then at last they were free to land on the bleak coast.

It seemed good to stand on solid earth again after the many

The Pilgrims landed at Plymouth in December, 1620

weeks of pitching about on the *Mayflower*. The men formed exploring parties, and the women took mountains of laundry ashore to wash. There had been no extra water for this purpose aboard ship. The girls helped their mothers and the boys dug clams and fished. But Francis and Johnny were disappointed. They had hoped to go with the men, but were told they were too young. The other children were not very friendly with the Billington boys, who were said to be lacking in religion. Moreover, their father was suspected of trying to start a mutiny on the voyage, so mothers warned their children against the two. Even their friends the dogs had gone with the men. The boys began to feel neglected and bored.

So they promptly got into trouble. They found some quills in a ship's cabin and made squibs, or firecrackers, by stuffing them with stolen gunpowder. They lighted these with a slow match — a piece of rope soaked in saltpeter — and set them off with a bang. It was fun until they were discovered. They had been playing right next to a keg of gunpowder, and it was a miracle that the whole *Mayflower* wasn't blown sky-high.

Now the boys were really in disgrace. Nobody would have anything to do with them. So they were overjoyed to learn that it had been decided to seek further for a good place to settle. The harbor at Provincetown was too shallow; there was no good water supply; and the men reported having had a fight with some Indians at First Encounter Beach. Francis and Johnny weren't surprised. A few days before, the men had

The women pounded corn into meal

found and brought back to the ship a large amount of corn and beans. The boys didn't blame the natives for being angry; but they were glad to leave the scene of their own troubles.

An exploring party reported that the best spot they could find was at what is now Plymouth, and when the Pilgrims arrived there it did seem a good place. There were a clear spring and a brook of pure water, a hill for a fort and lookout, cornfields already cleared, and meadows of hay along a salt river. The hay was very important, as it was to the early settlers what gasoline is to the farmers of today: fuel to run horse-power, and food for cattle as well. Without it there could be no animals for farming.

Here in Plymouth there were no Indians. They had all died

in an epidemic a few years before, leaving their cleared land and good cornfields for the first comers.

In the rush to get settled before snowfall, the colonists forgot the Billington boys' misdeeds. They and the other lads were set to digging clams, catching lobsters, and fishing. The better shots among the men were given the task of hunting deer and rabbits and wildfowl, for food was running low. The women and girls took some of the corn found near Provincetown and put it into heavy wooden bowls called mortars. Then they pounded it into meal with pestles, small blunt clubs, and baked it into flat cakes before open fires. Nobody liked this corn bread, but it was better than nothing. They called it journey cake at first, because it was handy to take on journeys; but they soon slipped into saying johnnycake.

For a while, at first, the women and children stayed on the *Mayflower,* which was anchored offshore, while the men were busy making shelters. With winter so close, they had to build what was quickest and easiest: probably rough huts made of branches and sod; or possibly dugouts — simply holes in the ground or in a hillside, roofed over with poles and bark. There were no chimneys. The fire was built on the dirt floor, and the smoke escaped through an opening in the roof. Or, at least, it was supposed to. More often than not, most of it stayed inside. These crude homes were damp, cold, and uncomfortable — little better than the dens of animals. But after the months on the crowded *Mayflower,* they seemed spacious and private to the colonists. One large common house for everyone was also built, made of clay and branches and with a thatch roof.

The discomfort didn't bother the boys as much as it would us. They, like all others of their time, were used to being uncomfortable. Even England's best homes were poorly heated. Everyone expected to be cold in winter, hot in summer, and wet when it rained. Raincoats and rubbers were unknown, as were lighter or heavier clothing for changing seasons. Cotton was rare and expensive, so clothes the year round were made of wool, linen, linsey-woolsey, or leather. In winter people added a coat or cape, and in summer even some of the grownups went barefoot, partly for comfort and partly to save their shoes.

The children dressed exactly like the grownups. Many of us think of the Pilgrims as always wearing black suits and tall stiff hats, or long dull gray dresses with white kerchiefs. On special occasions they did dress this way, but ordinarily they wore their work clothes, which were rather gay. The men and boys had warm knit Monmouth caps, like stocking caps, of red or blue or green to match their long wool stockings. Their knee breeches and leather jerkins were drab, but their shirts were blue, green, red, or yellow.

The women's clothes were colorful, too. They wore long full skirts and fitted bodices, like extra-wide belts, which laced over bright stomachers covering the front upper parts of their bodies. Sometimes they added little red vests for warmth, and big cloaks with gaily lined hoods. White caps kept their hair in place. They never wore jewelry, though — not even buckles — as this was against their religion. All in all, the whole company made a bright and cheerful picture as they worked on their new settlement under the gray New England sky.

For a month Francis and Johnny had a wonderful time. For fear of wolves and Indians they were not allowed to wander deep into the woods, though they were longing to explore them. However, they found plenty to keep them busy and amused in the town and along the shore. They climbed over the big rock where the small boats landed, helped with the building, and found starfish and odd shells while they were clamming.

They disliked Sundays. Although their family was not Separatist, they were obliged to observe the strict Pilgrim Sabbath, which lasted from sunset on Saturday until sunset on Sunday. During this time all play and all work, even the cooking of hot meals, was forbidden. The boys couldn't even take walks, as there was a law against "all sporting about the highways and fields." Worst of all from their viewpoint, they had to attend church in the common house in both the morning and the afternoon, and they had to pay attention to the two-hour sermon. The tithingman saw to it that they did. He stood at the back with a long stick in his hand. On one end was a squirrel's tail and on the other a hard wooden knob. Anyone who dozed was tickled awake with the tail, and anyone who did not pay attention was rapped smartly with the knob. Both boys received frequent raps.

In January the "Great Sickness" came

Although the settlers worried a great deal about Indians, none came into the village. But in January something worse than Indians attacked the colony — what was called the "Great Sickness." Almost everyone developed scurvy, a disease brought on by lack of the vitamins in fruit and vegetables. There were no native berries and greens at this time of year, and the Pilgrims had not eaten fresh fruit or vegetables for over four months. A great many of them, weakened by scurvy and unused to the harsh climate, hard labor, and miserable living conditions, fell ill with pneumonia. There was no penicillin, of course, and little other medicine, and no milk, eggs, or beef broth for the invalids. Almost every day two or three people died, and only six or seven were well enough to care for the others. Entire families were wiped out, and every family except the Billingtons lost some of its members. They escaped entirely, but the boys were often hungry and always tired from helping with all the work that fell on the shoulders of the healthy. It was a terrible time, enough to discourage the stoutest heart.

Fortunately, spring came early in 1621, and although half the colonists were dead the others slowly recovered as the sun climbed higher and the earth warmed. Their courage recovered, too, and when the *Mayflower* left for England not one of the settlers was aboard. With the warm weather Francis and Johnny were free to become acquainted with the countryside. They roamed the woods near the settlement, finding flowers strange to them — skunk's cabbage, lady's-slippers, and the delicate trailing arbutus, which the Pilgrims called the may-flower. The boys picked wild strawberries and climbed trees. From the top of one of the tallest, Francis spied a large body of water to the west. He ran home, excitedly shouting that he had discovered the Pacific Ocean. It turned out to be only a large pond, but to this day it is called Billington's Sea.

There was more work as well as more play, since the time for planting had come. Each family had a small kitchen garden for its own use, in which were planted the herbs and seeds brought from England. In addition, there was a big community cornfield just outside the village, where some of the corn found on the Cape was sown. Everyone cultivated this field, and the crop would be shared by everyone.

In addition to the planting, there was a great deal of building

The new homes seemed almost luxurious

to be done. The Pilgrims had no intention of spending another winter in their smoky, clammy dugouts. Since they had never heard of log cabins and did not know how to build them, they set about making small timber cottages like their old English homes.

This was a slow business. First they felled trees and trimmed them into logs. Then with a two-man crosscut saw they shaped the logs into squared timbers and rough planks. When enough had been sawed out, they started on a house.

English cottages did not have cellars. But the settlers had learned that New England winters were far more severe than those they were accustomed to and that cellars were necessary, both to keep the house warm and to provide a frostproof storage space for vegetables. So a cellar hole was dug and walled with stone. Then the chimney foundation and fireplace were built; for lack of cement, the stones were bound together with clay and mud. Last, the frame of the house was put together flat on the ground and the parts were joined with wooden pegs called treenails, or trunnels.

When everything was ready, all the men of the colony got together and lifted the frame into place. This was very hard work indeed, as they had no derricks or hoists but had to depend solely on their own muscles. But they managed. Long poles propped the building up until it could be made fast. After the frames had been boarded in, a roof of poles and thatch was put on and the cracks in the walls were filled with clay.

In contrast to the first rough shelters, these new homes seemed almost luxurious, but actually they were not very large and not at all comfortable, compared to the houses of today. Each had only one room with a large fireplace, and a small loft above, where the children slept. There were no rugs on the floors and no glass at the tiny windows; instead, greased paper let in a little light. Cold drafts came in through the chinks in the walls, and rain leaked through the thatch on the roof. Worse still, as the straw roofs dried, sparks from the chimneys often set them afire. Then everybody had to rush outdoors with the family belongings, no matter what the weather. Later, thatch roofs were not permitted because they were such a fire danger.

The furnishings were as simple as the houses. There had been no space on the *Mayflower* for shipping chairs, tables, and beds, so now the settlers made their own furniture. They nailed together rough slab stools and benches. Their beds, called jack-beds, were crude frames built into a corner, with rope for springs and big bags stuffed with feathers, rags, or even cattails for mattresses. The bigger children usually slept on the floor of the loft, and the small ones in trundle, or truckle, beds which could be shoved under the parents' big bed in the daytime to save space. Almost nobody made a table, as it, too, would take up too much room. The settlers ate off benches or their knees.

Even in Europe there was very little iron or other metal in use at this time, and the colonists had to use wood in place of it whenever possible. Meals were served on wooden plates or trenchers, with wooden spoons. There was a long iron fork for toasting, but no table forks. Instead, the settlers used their fingers, and they used their hunting knives for cutting meat. No one had table linen or china, silver, and glass. They drank out of wooden mugs called noggins, or tankards made of boiled leather and called blackjacks. Even bottles were made of leather. Only those utensils which were put directly over the fire were of the precious iron.

These cooking utensils were a spider, or frying pan; a saucepan; a gridiron, or broiler; perhaps an iron pot or two; and a large kettle with a close-fitting cover, called a bake-kettle. The utensils often had long handles and three legs about four inches long, so that they could be set in the coals of the fireplace without burning the food in them. The bake-kettle could be used for stews and soups, but it could also be used as an oven. Johnny-cake batter could be poured into it and covered tightly, and the whole thing could be buried in the hot coals and ashes of the fireplace. After a while the coals were raked away, the cover taken off, and there was the corn bread, all nicely browned.

Roasts were cooked on a spit, or long rod, thrust through the meat and hung over the fire. A few people had iron spits, but most of them had to use green wood. At the end of the rod was a crank, and someone — usually one of the children — had to sit and turn the spit slowly and constantly so that the meat would cook evenly. This was a very tiresome job, and Johnny and Francis hated it. They wished their mother would always serve the stew that she cooked in her largest iron pot, since they were not expected to attend to that.

Everyone kept a stewpot going, from time to time adding scraps of meat and, when possible, vegetables and boiling the stew every day. This boiling was necessary to keep it from spoiling, since there were no iceboxes. The stews were rich and nourishing, and were one of the chief foods.

The same large kettle was used for two other necessary household chores: the making of soap and the dipping of candles. For both of these products all household fats and greases were carefully saved. To make candles, tallow was melted in the kettle, but not allowed to become too hot. Then five or six strings attached to a rod were dipped in it and hung on a rack to cool. When the grease was firm, they were dipped again and again, until the candles were of the proper thickness. Candle-making was a tiresome job, and the candles smelled terrible when they were burned. Later the settlers found that much better candles could be made from the wax of the gray bayberries that grew along the beach. They not only gave a clearer light, but they smelled good, too.

Soap-making was even harder work and had to be done outdoors, because of the horrible smell. For weeks before soap-making day, all the wood ashes from the fire were collected in a barrel of straw and water. Soaking them made lye, which was drained off through a small hole in the bottom of the barrel.

The women dipped candles

Then the lye and grease were boiled together and stirred constantly in one direction only. Finally the mixture thickened into a harsh soft soap which was very rough for the hands, but did get clothes clean.

The lye barrel was made of wood, as all other barrels and buckets were. Instead of being bound with metal, as ours are, they were hooped with tough hickory or ash switches. All the hinges and latches of doors were wooden, too, and even the spades, rakes, and hoes used in the gardens were whittled out of wood. That was one thing plentiful in the New World. But preparing a garden for seeding with only a blunt wooden shovel to use must have been very difficult.

With the coming of spring, the first Indian visited the town. His name was Samoset. A few days later, having found that the

English were friendly, he came back with a friend, Tisquantum or Squanto, a man with an interesting history.

He had always lived at Plymouth until about fifteen years before, when he had gone to England with an explorer and stayed for ten years. Soon after his return to Plymouth, he had been kidnapped by a villainous sea captain and sold into slavery in Spain. Later he had escaped to England and then made his way back to the coast of Maine. When he finally arrived in Plymouth again, he found that his whole tribe had been wiped out by disease. So he had gone to live with Massasoit's tribe nearby. He was too homesick to be happy there, however, and almost at once he moved in with the Pilgrims and never left them again. He was worth a thousand times his weight in gold to them. He spoke English well; he understood English customs; he was familiar with every pebble in Plymouth; and he knew tricks of living there that the colonists might never have learned by themselves.

He taught them, for example, where and how to fish by Indian methods: especially how to trap the alewives that ran up the brook in the spring to spawn. He knew what wild herbs and greens were good to eat and, most important of all, how to raise a good corn crop. Corn then and for a long time to come was not only the chief food, but a substitute for money as well. Money was of no use in the wilderness, but good corn would buy almost anything one needed, either from the Indians or from other colonies.

Squanto showed the Pilgrims how to plant corn

Corn should not be planted in rows, Squanto said, but in hills a few feet apart. For fertilizer in each hill three of the alewives should be buried, placed like the spokes of a wheel, with their heads together in the center. The proper time for planting was when the oak leaves were the size of a mouse's ear. Pumpkins planted between the hills shaded the ground with their big leaves, keeping it moist and discouraging weeds. If beans were planted in the corn hills, the cornstalks could be made to serve as bean poles. The Pilgrims followed his directions, and had an excellent corn crop in the fall.

Squanto was fond of children and soon he had every boy in the village at his heels. He told them stories about the animals, showed them how to make traps and snares and how to skin and dress game, and taught them a few Indian words and customs. They learned as much of value from him as they ever would have in school, and it was more fun. The other parts of schooling — the three R's — were taught children by their parents as best they were able. Since some grownups could neither read nor write very well and none had much spare time for teaching, school was not a great burden to Plymouth boys and girls.

Squanto also introduced the Pilgrim leaders to Massasoit, sachem or chief of the local Wampanoags. He and the settlers made a peace treaty which was kept for fifty-four years. It bound each party to help the other in emergencies.

Johnny Billington, who was now seven, caused the first emergency. He lost himself in the woods. For five days he wandered about, while the whole colony searched for him. Finally, hungry, tired, and scared, he reached an Indian village twenty miles away, on Cape Cod. The Indians fed him and took him on to the Nauset tribe, far down the Cape — the very tribe with whom the Pilgrims had fought at First Encounter Beach. By this time the men of Plymouth had decided that they could waste no more time looking for a boy who was probably dead anyhow; but they asked Massasoit to inquire for Johnny among the tribes. Massasoit soon learned where he was.

Governor Carver ordered a small boat, or shallop, to go around the Cape and bring Johnny home. Everyone was rather

A shallop went to bring Johnny home

disgusted by all this fuss, but the affair turned out very well. The Governor thought that since they had to make the trip anyhow, they might as well take this opportunity to pay the Nausets for the corn they had taken in December. This act of fairness led to a peace treaty and ended fear of Indian attack for a long time to come. Johnny's adventure was of real service to the colony.

Johnny himself enjoyed it very much. He came home all dressed up in wampum beads and talked of nothing else all summer. The other boys grew very tired of hearing him brag. It wasn't until fall that attention was turned to another matter.

By this time everyone was in good health. The new cabins

were finished and snug, and stores of fish, game, berries, and corn had been salted or dried against the coming winter. The Pilgrims felt that they had done well in the short time they had been at Plymouth, and that they should give thanks to God for His mercy to them. When Massasoit and ninety of his tribe came through the bright-leaved autumn woods to pay a fall visit, the settlers decided to hold a feast. The Indians made a gift of five deer and some wild turkeys, and great fires were built in the open to cook them. The Pilgrim women made corn bread and huge kettles of a food Squanto had taught them to make, called succotash. This was a rich stew of meat and wild fowl, to which large amounts of corn and beans were added. Trestle tables were set up outdoors for the meal, although the Indians preferred to sit on the ground. After Elder Brewster had asked a blessing, everyone fell to heartily.

This was the first time the Indian women and children had visited Plymouth, and after the first shyness had worn off they began to enjoy themselves. The brown and the white women compared clothes and babies, and the children ran races and played games. The men held shooting matches with guns against bows and arrows. Everyone had such a good time that the guests stayed for three days. That was the first Thanksgiving.

The second winter was not as bad as the first. Now the colonists knew what to expect and were better prepared. A few hens had been brought over from England on a later ship, and young turkeys had been caught and tamed to start turkey flocks. The storehouse contained a few peas, parsnips, and turnips from English seed, as well as the native corn and beans. And Squanto had taught the settlers to make maple syrup and maple sugar. Because of the better balanced diet there was no sickness that winter, aside from a few colds and sniffles.

In spite of the preparations, however, the settlers did run short of corn. As it happened, the *Discovery* had sailed up from Virginia earlier with a load of beads and knives which the Pilgrims bought. With these to trade, they sailed the shallop back to Johnny's friends the Nausets and secured twenty-six barrels of corn and beans. But it proved to be an unlucky voyage. Squanto, who had gone with them, became ill and died on the way, and the shallop was driven high onto the shore at Yarmouth on the return trip. The men had to hide the corn and walk fifty miles home. Later Myles Standish and a party went back and rescued both the boat and the food.

The leaders learned a lesson from the shortage of corn. They decided that people would work harder on land of their own than they would on that which belonged to everyone. The following spring, instead of having one enormous cornfield for the whole colony, they gave out to each family a plot of its own outside the village. Here each could grown its private store of corn. This made a tremendous difference. Francis and Johnny and their mother who, like all the other women and children, had always looked for excuses not to work in the cornfield now

43

In the spring a bull and two heifers came

became very much interested in raising the largest crop possible. The hard work, too, took their minds off the loss of Squanto, whom they missed terribly.

Under this new plan, in spite of a dry summer, there was enough corn to see the settlement through the winter. In the spring the *Charity* arrived from England with a bull and three heifers, as well as a good supply of clothing. Everyone had been running around in rags and patches for a long time, so this cargo was very welcome. And so was the prospect of milk and butter.

The crop that fall was excellent. Not only did the Pilgrims have enough corn for themselves, but some to spare. This they traded with the Indians for furs to pay for necessary goods from England.

Thanksgiving that year was a truly joyous occasion. At last the Pilgrims felt that they were getting ahead. They had been at Plymouth only three years, but already they were self-supporting. Sixteen-year-old Jamestown had cost a great deal of money and thousands of lives and was still dependent on England for support. The settlers were not so foolish as to think that all their troubles were over and that everything was going to be smooth sailing from then on. But they believed that they had overcome the worst difficulties and that they would be equal to any others that would arise.

Best of all, they now felt at home in the New World. They had grown to love the countryside and to find the climate invigorating rather than cruel. They enjoyed the outdoor life, the freedom of the woods and beaches, and the sense of accomplishing something by their own efforts. Francis and Johnny could hardly remember what it had been like in England. They, like the others, looked forward rather than back. They didn't realize it, but deep inside they were already beginning to think of themselves as Americans.

4

THE DUTCH AT NEW AMSTERDAM

While the Virginians were trying to start a colony and get rich quickly with the least possible effort in Jamestown, and while the Pilgrims were patiently working out a new way of life for themselves in Plymouth, the Dutch were busy on the Hudson River. Unlike the Venturers, they had no dreams of a Northwest Passage to the Indies or of gold mines; and unlike the Pilgrims, they had in the beginning no idea of a permanent settlement. They came in 1613 simply to trade with the Indians. It was not until more than ten years later that a real colony began to grow at Fort Amsterdam, where New York City now stands.

In 1626, partly because of political and religious unrest in Holland, a group of thirty families emigrated to Fort Amsterdam. These settlers brought with them cattle and horses, sheep and pigs, all carefully tended during the voyage so that they arrived in good condition. The Dutch were the best prepared of all the groups who sought homes in the New World.

But settling in a strange, wild land is never easy, even for the well prepared. At first the colonists lived in rude dugouts or rough bark huts clustered around a small palisaded fort which was used more as a trading center than for defense. At that time they had little or no trouble with the Indians, whom they treated as business acquaintances.

Because the Dutch liked to eat well and were really more interested in trading than in farming or hunting, they made sure that plenty of food was sent from Holland. To be sure, it was neither very appetizing nor very exciting. One early settler wrote to friends in Holland that the rations, which were given out by the Company, were "hard stale food, and the wild things were unfit to gather." However, getting supplies was easier for the Dutch than it had been for the Venturers or the Pilgrims, because ships from the Dutch West India Company were constantly coming into the harbor to pick up cargoes of beaver and other furs. The colonists may have been bored and homesick at times, but they never really suffered the cold and hunger that plagued the other settlers.

Beaver fur was the chief interest of the colony, and not necessarily new beaver fur at that. The traders bought bundles of filthy old wraps, called matchcoats, that the Indians had discarded. The reason for this purchase was the tremendous demand all over Europe for beaver hats. A beaver hat was actually a felt hat, and the felt was made of the soft underfur of beaver

47

Beaver fur was the chief interest of the colony

skins. Other furs could be used, but beaver was best; and old fur from which the long stiff guard hairs had been worn was best of all. Beaver hats were very expensive, but a good one would last fifty or sixty years, and very often a man would write special directions into his will, leaving his beaver hat to a favorite son or close friend. It was on this fashion that the first little settlement of Fort Amsterdam rested. Even now, when it is known as New York City, much of its business still depends on fashion.

For a long time after its beginning the colony suffered its ups-and-downs: poor directors; too many traders compared to the number of people who wanted really to make farms and homes; misunderstandings with the Indians; and all the other worrisome difficulties that are part of settling a new land. But gradually times grew better. There was more variety in the food; the huts began to be replaced by wooden houses; the settlers began to feel that the New World was their home.

It was many years, however, before genuine prosperity came. Then the Dutch *really* felt at home; they raised houses like those they had known in Holland. Some of these were built of red or yellow brick, either imported from the old country or made in the new. But more of the houses were built mostly of wood, with brick ends, one of which usually faced the street. The houses themselves were high and narrow, with the end walls rising above the roof level and finished in steps rather

Dutch houses in Manhattan

View of early Manhattan

than a straight slope. Often the bricks were laid in fancy patterns and the initials of the owner or the date of the building were worked into the wall. The roofs had a very steep pitch, so that there were two attics, the lower used for sleeping and the upper, called the cockloft, used for storage. At first the roofs were of thatch, but as soon as possible the thatch, because it caught fire easily, was replaced by curved red tiles.

These houses, grouped about a wooden church, a windmill, the fort, and a brewery, formed a little town. Farther up the island, farms were laid out to help supply the needs of the village. They were so neat that they looked almost unreal. The rows of vegetables were perfectly straight, with not a weed to be seen; the orchards were trim and well pruned; and the beautiful cows were scrubbed and spotless. Men farmed this way in Holland, and they saw no excuse for lowering their standards in the wilderness. The houses of the farmers were different from those of the townsmen. They were low, built of stone or clapboard, with gently pitched overhanging roofs of shingle or thatch, much like the farmhouses of the Flemish countryside.

Three things about the Dutch town houses were new not only to America, but to English builders as well. Later they were commonly adopted, and we still use two of them very often. The first thing was the Dutch door, which is split crossways in the middle so that the sections swing separately. A Dutch housewife could open the top half to speak to callers or ventilate her house and still leave the bottom half shut, with no danger of a toddler running into the street or of cats, dogs, or hens wandering in.

Outside the door was an uncovered platform called a *stoep,* which we pronounce stoop. A high-backed bench was built on each side of it, and here Dutch families sat in pleasant weather when their work was done — the women mending, the men smoking their long pipes, and the children whispering secrets. Everybody who went by paused to chat; it made a nice ending to a busy day. The *stoep* was the beginning of our porches.

The Dutch houses, like all early houses, were without dining rooms. One large family room served as kitchen, dining room, and living room. But the larger Dutch houses had something unheard of elsewhere: a parlor. This was the "best" room, shut up except on special occasions such as weddings or funerals. Later the idea spread all over the Northeast, so that most people who could afford it had one of these rooms, closed tight most of the time and full of stiff furniture. Some still exist in the back country of New England; but nowadays most people feel that houses are supposed to be lived in and used, and that a parlor is rather silly.

Another room set aside in many houses was far from silly. It was a shop where all sorts of small goods, food, and other necessities were sold to the neighbors, to the ships that came in from other colonies, and to the Indians. The Dutch had come to trade, and trade they were bound to do. Since the man of the

The Dutch used wampum in trading

house was often out on business, the shops were tended by the housewife or one of the older children.

Tending shop was not as simple as it sounds. None of the goods had prices marked on them. The shopkeeper tried to get as much pay for an article as possible. He would ask far too large an amount to start with, and the customer would laugh and say that was ridiculous — and it was. Then, in turn, the customer would offer too little. Each person understood the other perfectly, and they both knew that they would end somewhere in the middle. To us this seems a foolish way to do business, but it was very good training in values for boys who would grow up to be traders. They made mistakes, of course, and sold things at a loss sometimes. But they seldom made the same mistake twice.

There was a great scarcity of small silver and copper coins, so something had to take their place in doing business. In Virginia, corn in the early days and later tobacco was used as money; and in Plymouth, corn. In New Amsterdam neither of these was especially rare and valuable, so they could not serve successfully as payment. Oddly enough, wampum filled the need.

Wampum is nothing but shell beads. It comes in two colors, white and purple, and is usually made from hard clam or oyster shells. The shell is mostly white, but near the hinge is a small spot of purple. Many white beads can be made from one shell, but only a few purple; hence the purple beads were more valuable. Moreover, the shells could be found only along the coast, and the work of making the beads was long and fussy. About the same amount of time was needed to manufacture a reasonably long string of wampum as to trap ten beaver, so the Indians were accustomed to swapping skins or corn or arrow flints for wampum. The Dutch took over this practice, and it was not at all unusual for a mother to send her little daughter to the store in the home of a neighbor with a string of wampum, as mothers today give their children dimes and quarters, to pay for a pound of sugar or a skein of yarn.

Dutch housewives were probably the best in the world. Their houses were always spotless. They scrubbed not only the floors and the woodwork, but the ceilings, outside doors, and porch steps as well; and they did it at least once a week. After their

The women used brooms made of splintered birch logs

floors were bone-white, they sprinkled them with clean sand to protect them. When they swept up the sand, all other dust and dirt came with it. In the sand of the parlor floor, which was not walked on much, they often traced designs, so that it looked like a carpet.

All this sweeping used up a great many brooms. Quite a few men earned extra money by broom-making. They took a birch log about five inches thick and six feet long, and with a sharp knife shredded the end into very fine splinters fourteen or fifteen inches long. Then, working in the other direction, they whittled other splinters until the broomstick was slim enough to handle. They bent the second lot of splinters downward over the bushy end they had first made and tied them securely with stout twine. This made a fine broom, although it was a little heavy. But Dutch women were strong and energetic and didn't mind a heavy broom.

Besides being wonderful housekeepers, they were also excellent cooks. Like all colonial women, they cooked at an open fire in the family room. Their fireplaces were taller and shallower than those in other places, and often they were bordered with blue and white tiles. Because New Amsterdam, as it was now called, was first and foremost a trading town, the Dutch could get luxuries like tiles easily. They could also have china dishes, and pewter mugs and porringers and plates which they kept brightly polished with wood ashes and oil and displayed on shelves. The same ships that brought these goods brought

56

The Dutch found many ways to cook Indian corn

spices and raisins and oranges and lemons, so that Dutch food was much more interesting than that of other colonies.

For example, the women made a sort of doughnut full of citron, orange peel, raisins, and spice, which they fried in deep fat. They loved sweet cakes and fritters and crullers, too. They had a cooking utensil unknown in other settlements: a long-handled waffle iron which they filled with rich batter and held over the coals. The crisp golden waffles were drenched with butter and eaten hot. The Dutch liked butter and had made sure they would have plenty by bringing with them good milk-giving cows. From the milk they also made huge cheeses, which they grated and sprinkled over many foods.

They found ways to dress up even the Indian corn that all settlers in the New World depended on to a large extent. Instead of the plain hasty pudding that the others made, they cooked their corn meal in milk, added ginger and molasses, and made a dish like our Indian pudding. Or they simmered corn meal in water and added beef, pork, venison, or wild fowl, along with turnips, carrots, and onions. This they cooked slowly on the very edge of the fire for three days. By then it was so thick that it could be turned out of the kettle in a loaf, which was sliced and eaten hot; or, after it was cold, could be fried in big slabs.

It is not surprising, considering their rich and enormous meals, that the Dutch needed larger and stronger furniture than other colonists. But their weight wasn't the only thing they considered. They liked to be comfortable, and they shipped from Holland heavy chairs with leather seats and wide, convenient arms.

Besides wanting to be comfortable, they loved to be neat; they had not only the chests that all colonists brought, but tall wardrobes as well, in which they hung their clothes. No untidy-looking garments on pegs in the wall for the Dutch! They kept even their beds out of sight, building them like bunks into the walls and concealing them with curtains or folding doors. They slept on great fluffy feather beds into which they sank deep, and in cold weather they covered themselves with lighter feather puffs.

As time went on, the clothes of the town dwellers became rather stylish. Though the farmers dressed in sturdy work clothes, the men of the town wore baggy pantaloons; on their heads were wide-brimmed hats with curling plumes, and on their feet fine leather shoes with carefully worked ornamental buckles. They liked the starched and pleated collars called ruffs, which were hard to launder — but the Dutch women were equal to the task.

In general, the town women dressed fashionably. Their clothes were bright, because they liked color. Over several striped petticoats they wore rather shorter skirts than did the Pilgrim women, to show their embroidered stockings. Their tight bodices were covered with loose, short-sleeved jackets, and on their heads were little quilted caps of linen print.

But one thing about their costumes gave a clue to their industry. No matter how elegant her finery, each Dutch woman wore around her waist a narrow girdle from which hung on ribbons or chains a number of objects which she liked to have handy. There were her scissors and pincushion and a small purse holding hanks of thread. She was prepared to mend a torn blouse immediately, without wasting time looking for her sewing kit. The keys to her chests and storeroom hung on another chain, and still another ended in her knitting bag. Whenever she sat down, she did a few more rows on the cap or scarf that she was making. She hated wasting time so much that often she would knit as she walked along the street to the store or to call on a friend.

Dutch youngsters dressed much as their parents did, except

that they wore wooden shoes. These lasted a long time and were easy to replace when they were outgrown. The children took them off when they entered the house and left them in a row on the *stoep*. Indoors they wore felt slippers to save their mothers' floors from hard wear.

After the first years of hardship the New Amsterdam children had a much gayer time than Pilgrim children did. All the Dutch loved parties and made great events of weddings, birthdays, and holidays. At these parties games were played, including kissing games, which would have been viewed with horror in Plymouth. The Dutch wanted their children to have fun and in fact rather spoiled them. Unlike the Pilgrims, they had a number of holidays which they celebrated.

Sometime in December came First Skating Day. That was the day when the ice was officially declared safe for skaters. Then everyone strapped on skates and whizzed up and down the river, cutting circles and figure eights and showing off in general. Back in Holland skating was almost a national sport, and the Dutch brought it along with them. The children also brought another pastime: coasting on sleds.

On December 6 Sant Nikolaas came, and left gifts for good boys and girls. His servant, Black Ruprecht, was supposed to accompany him to punish those who had been naughty during the year, but the fond Dutch parents were apt to forget mischief on this feast day and gradually Black Ruprecht himself was forgotten, too.

Almost at once came New Year's Day, when everybody kept open house. People drifted from dwelling to dwelling, making New Year's calls, eating too much and having a wonderful time. Then there was May Day, when maypoles were set up and there was dancing on the green; and Pinkster Day, brought over from the old country — a time for jokes and tricks, like our Halloween.

But perhaps the best fun of all for little Dutch boys was wandering down to the canal to watch the *vlie* boats come in with their cargoes of fur from Fort Orange up the river. These *vlie* boats were little sloops suitable for river travel. Once they arrived in New Amsterdam, they discharged their loads, which were priced and reloaded on the big ocean-going ships.

The canal, together with the windmill and the brick houses, made New Amsterdam as much as possible like the old country. Later, when the English took over New Amsterdam and renamed it New York, they filled in the canal; it is now Broad Street.

But in the olden days it was a pleasant, busy place. The little boys could sit in the sun, dangling their feet in wooden shoes over the quiet water, and watching the unloading. They saw bearded trappers and half-naked Indians and listened to the talk of the men who worked on the boats. They had a fine time and went home with their heads full of tales of the back country. Then they ate their suppers and went to bed in their bunks, where they heard hourly the report of the rattle-watch.

The rattle-watch was the first civilian police force in America. Its members walked the little streets at night, watching out for fires, thievery, or any other breaking of the peace, just as our night officers do. Every hour they were also obliged to report the weather, and the time, as measured by an hourglass. Before they made their announcement they swung their rattles — wooden objects with a stick that clattered on a cogged wheel, like a party noise-maker.

Then little Dutch children, awakened by the rattle, could hear the watchman's voice ring out, "Twelve o'clock, full moon, and all is well." Or on a nasty night, "Two by the glass and a storm of sleet." Then the boys and girls, warm and safe between their feather beds, would curl themselves into tighter knots, glad that they were not out in the cold and the dark and the slashing sleet which they could hear beating against their windows.

After a time, the Dutch lost New Amsterdam to the English, but they left their mark on America. There are the names of both families and places; the doughnut, which is now almost a national dish; and the Dutch door and the stoop. We know Sant Nikolaas as Santa Claus. And the little town which they built on lower Manhattan is still America's greatest trade center.

5

THE SWEDES AT FORT CHRISTINA

Probably the best colonists of all were the Swedes and Finns who settled in the Delaware Valley in 1638. For a long time King Gustavus Adolphus of Sweden, tired of the continual fighting in Europe, had had dreams of a Swedish colony in the New World where, as he himself said, "the laborer should reap the fruit of his toil, where the rights of conscience should be inviolate, an asylum for the persecuted, a place of security." Of all the reasons for colonizing, these given so long ago by the Swedish king come nearest to what Americans like to believe their country represents today: freedom to think, work, and worship as they please, without fear.

However, Gustavus Adolphus died before he could make his dream come true, and his daughter Christina came to the throne. As she was only a little girl, control of the country was really in the hands of her ministers. They agreed that the old king's plan should be tried, especially as most of the other major

The Indians were snaring shad

European countries now had colonies in America; but they had trouble persuading people to undertake this venture. The Swedish were contented in their orderly country and had no wish to leave it.

Finally, however, in the springtime of 1638, a party of twenty-three Swedish soldiers aboard two ships, the *Kalmar Nyckel* and the *Grip,* sailed into the broad mouth of the Delaware River, which had been named for Lord De la Warr of Virginia. All along the banks dogwood, laurel, and tulip trees were in bloom, filling the air with sweetness. Behind them rose forests of pine, oak, walnut, and many other hardwoods, hung with looping grapevines; and close to the ground grew beach plum and huckleberry bushes. The land-wise Swedish saw at once that here was a fine, fertile, and bountiful land, where a living could easily be made.

It was the time of the first run of shad, and the river was crowded with the canoes of the local Minqua Indians, who were snaring the fish with grapevine nets. Along the banks stood their lodges, where the squaws were smoking the catches over hickory-wood fires in preparation for the winter. Peter Minuit, the leader of the expedition, thought it best not to crowd the Indians and so start possible trouble, and he directed the ships farther upriver to a rocky point where Wilmington, Delaware, now stands. Here at the rocks the soldiers landed and set about building their little town, which they called Fort Christina in honor of their queen. They had been instructed to buy the land

A stockade of logs was built

from the Indians in exchange for merchandise, and this Peter Minuit did, as he had done years earlier for Fort Amsterdam.

In this connection, a look at the ships' cargo is interesting. It included several thousand yards of cloth; several hundred axes, hatchets, and adzes; several hundred knives; dozens of tobacco pipes; mirrors and looking glasses; gilded chains and finger rings; and combs, earrings, and other ornaments for the Indians. Spades, hoes, and other tools for use in starting the colony were also on board.

As in all settlements, the problem of shelter and protection came first, and a stockade of logs was erected. Then Peter Minuit gave out different tasks to different groups. Some were set to preparing and planting gardens, and others were asked to make dwellings. It was impossible to make good houses at first, so the men probably lived in rough shelters dug in the ground and roofed with sod; or they may have made wigwam-like tents of branches and the skins of animals, as they had seen the Laplanders do. These men were not real colonizers; they were soldiers; and Fort Christina at first was a trading post. When the ships sailed for home, however, word went with them that farmers and real settlers were needed.

But again, most people were contented and did not wish to risk life in an unknown land. Finally, in desperation, the authorities hit on a scheme. They would give their lawbreakers a choice. Either they could go overseas to colonize, or they must serve army duty or be severely punished, possibly by death. Most of the guilty ones chose colonizing.

A colony of lawbreakers does not sound like a very safe or happy place; but here are some of the crimes of which these early settlers were guilty. One man had been imprisoned for climbing over a wall and cutting down six apple trees — heaven knows why. Others were convicted for shooting deer and elk and using only their hides, leaving their meat to rot on the ground. Still others were accused of being weather-witches — people who forecast the weather with suspicious accuracy. Then there were those who were uncannily skillful in locating underground water with the aid of peeled peach forks, which they held in their hands until the end of the twig bent to the ground, showing where to dig a well. Everyone agreed that these men and the weather-witches must be in league with the Devil, and because of their activities were not desirable citizens.

But the worst offenders of all were the Finns — the forest-destroying Finns, as they were called. Their crime was cutting down trees and burning over wooded areas in order to plant gardens in the clearings. This was very much against the law, so the Finns were given the same choice as the other criminals. All these lawless characters were obliged to take their wives and children with them; as a result, the Swedish settlement became, like Plymouth, a community of families.

No better group of colonists could have been chosen. What had been crimes in Sweden became valuable skills and abilities on the Delaware. There people were needed who liked to cut down trees and to plant crops, who could find water and foretell the weather. These men were not criminals at all; they were simply out of step with the ways of civilized Sweden. On the Delaware River they found the life to which they were suited.

The wild Finns, especially, had the true feeling of pioneers. They had cleared land and built many, many forest dwellings at home and they erected the same kind on the Delaware. These were the first real log cabins in America.

To make a cabin, the Finns cut logs of even lengths and notched them near the ends. Then they piled one log on another, in the form of a square, with the notches fitting so closely that only very small cracks were left between the logs. These were filled with a mixture of clay, moss, and chips. Small windows were cut and covered with sliding boards which could

A Finnish log cabin

be opened or closed, and a low door was hung on leather hinges. At the very first, a hole in the roof served to let out smoke from the fire, but later a huge, clay-plastered chimney was built on one wall. The roof was covered with bark or thatch, and the floor was made of dirt.

Log cabins like this were rather dark and cramped, but they were the best possible frontier dwellings. They could be built of material that had to be cut anyhow to clear the land, and only an ax was needed as a tool. No framework or nails were necessary. In a pinch, a man could build a cabin alone. The thick walls kept dwellers warm in winter and cool in summer. So good and practical were these houses that later other pioneers, going westward, copied them. To many people the log cabin has come to stand for American frontier life; it was the Swedes and Finns at Fort Christina who introduced it to this continent.

The furnishings of the cabins were crude — benches and three-legged stools made of slabs with the bark side down. Later, jack-beds were built into the corners, but at first the settlers slept on piles of leaves and grass on the dirt floor. There was too much to be done to waste time on luxuries like beds. Building a lean-to onto the cabin for storage or a workshop was more important, or worrying the stumps out of the cleared land and getting crops started.

To do this hard labor the Swedish and Finns needed hearty food. Daily they ate four big meals, made up of good solid food

The furnishings of the cabins were crude

like venison, bear meat, or wildfowl, and vegetables — beans, peas, corn, turnips, and onions. This was a hard-working community, for it received very little help from the old country, but on the whole it was a happy place.

Among the settlers' great sources of enjoyment were the great log *bastus* which they built on the riverbank. These were tightly sealed steam bathhouses with enormous fireplaces, and double tiers of bunks built around the walls.

Several hours before bathing time, a roaring fire was built in the fireplace and was kept going until the hut was breathlessly hot. When the bathers came, they lay naked in the upper bunks for a while, perspiring freely. Then the women who served as bath attendants poured buckets of water on the red-hot stones of the fireplace, until the *bastu* was filled with steam. The bathers moved to the lower bunks, where they lay gasping for breath while the attendants switched them with slender birch branches or scoured them with stiff twig brushes. At last, their pores clean and their blood circulating quickly, the bathers rushed outdoors and plunged into the cold river or in winter rolled naked in the snow. This was rather rugged treatment, but the Swedish and Finns enjoyed it, and it kept their bodies well-toned and free from fat. They were the only early settlers who bathed regularly all year round.

They sang a great deal, too, getting together in groups almost like choral societies and rollicking through the folk songs of the old country. They liked good music and passed laws to avoid having to listen to the other kind. Anyone who had a harsh voice was obliged by law to keep still or sing very softly; everybody was forbidden "to sing as if they were calling cows"; and there was a five shilling fine for "untimely singing," such as bellowing songs in the middle of the night.

From the very beginning these colonists were on good terms with the Indians. Both parties wanted only to be let alone to attend to their own affairs. Only once, in the very first days, was there an alarm. At that time the settlers were not sure they could trust the Minquas, so they kept a night-long watch. One night the guard roused the fort by beating the drum and shouting, "Awake! The enemy is all about us!"

Everyone rushed to the walls and, sure enough, they could

The settlers spread out from the fort

see lights burning on all sides. For hours the whole garrison stood at alert, waiting for the attack. Finally someone braver than the rest stole quietly out and discovered that the lights were only fireflies, unknown in Sweden, winking in the bushes and grass.

As soon as it was clear that the Minquas meant them no harm, the settlers began to spread out from the fort, building log cabins in clearings all along the river. They did their traveling to and fro in small boats along this natural highway. On their little farms they raised wheat and flax, and sowed meadows of European grass seed for their flocks and herds. It was they who introduced peach trees to this continent; the peach blossom is today the state flower of Delaware.

The Minquas, who were an agricultural people themselves, understood and respected the efforts of the colonists. They recognized good farmers when they met them. Soon the two peoples, the red and the white, were on truly neighborly terms. The Indians taught the white women how best to cure and fashion furs and how to make moccasins. They often bought surplus produce from the settlers and paid for it with beaver skins. The thrifty Swedish housewives, busy as they were with cooking the huge meals, caring for their children, spinning, weaving, and making into garments the flax and wool from the farms, found time to fashion little articles that the Indians liked, and traded them for furs and corn. Especially popular were short, gay embroidered vests and little knit caps with long bright tassels. The Indians, who had known only corn bread, loved the crisp brown loaves of white bread that came out of the brick ovens; so the women made and sold these, too. They did everything possible to help their husbands succeed in the New World.

In Sweden at this time it was considered a disgrace even to country people if their children could not read and write, and a system of education had been planned even before the colonists left home. Queen Christina and her ministers ordered particularly that "the patrons of this colony shall be obliged at all times to support as many schoolmasters as the number of inhabitants shall seem to require." Since the farms were scattered, it was impossible to have a school convenient to everyone. Instead, a traveling teacher went from place to place, boarding with whatever family he happened to be visiting.

On his first trip he laid out the lessons to be mastered before his next visit. These were taught by the parents or grown children to the younger ones. When the teacher came again, he drilled and tested the pupils very severely and was not satisfied with half-learned lessons. Then he made suggestions for improvement and laid out the next section of work to be done. This he would hear on his next trip.

But hard as the settlers and their children worked, and prosperous as they seemed at times, fate was against them. In Sweden it was never easy to find settlers for the New World colony and sometimes two years passed before supplies could be sent from home. During the seventeen years of their colonizing, the Swedish never had more than a few hundred settlers along the Delaware.

It was possibly because their settlement was so orderly, industrious, and peaceable that it lasted less than twenty years. The Dutch, who lived not far to the north, were beginning to settle along the Delaware, too. They saw the rich lands of the Swedish colonists and were envious of them. In 1655 Peter Stuyvesant, the governor of New Amsterdam, sent a large fleet of heavily armed vessels to occupy Fort Christina. The Swedish had no army and no battleships; they had never needed them. They were forced to surrender without a struggle.

But while they might from that time be considered as Dutch subjects, they continued their daily life as usual. They farmed their land, took their steam baths, and held their song festivals. Their way of life did not change completely for a long time, and some of the things they brought with them still exist as a part of our own lives today.

All of the early colonies left their legacies to modern America. Some of the settlers came for greed, some for excitement, some to better their position in the world, and some for religious freedom or to escape punishment. Some conducted themselves foolishly and some wisely in the beginning. Yet each brought something of value that has remained. Perhaps the most valuable thing of all was the example they set of courage and initiative — good, plain get-up-and-go; it has come to be recognized as a true American heritage.

OTHER BOOKS TO READ

AULAIRE, INGRI D' AND EDGAR PARIN *Pocahontas*. Doubleday & Company, Inc., 1949

DAUGHERTY, JAMES HENRY *Landing of the Pilgrims*. Random House, 1950

HALL-QUEST, OLGA *Jamestown Adventure*. E. P. Dutton & Co., Inc., 1950

MALOY, LOIS AND ALICE DALGLIESH *Wooden Shoes in America*. Charles Scribner's Sons, 1940. o.p.

MORISON, SAMUEL ELIOT *Story of the "Old Colony" of New Plymouth, 1620-1692*. Alfred A. Knopf, Inc., 1956

ACKNOWLEDGMENT

In preparing this account of the early settlements, the author has found many books most helpful, among them the following especially:

ANDREWS, MATTHEW PAGE *The Soul of a Nation.* Charles Scribner's Sons, 1943

BRADFORD, WILLIAM *Of Plymouth Plantation,* with notes and an introduction by Samuel Eliot Morison. Alfred A. Knopf, Inc., 1952.

HOWE, HENRY F. *Salt Rivers of the Massachusetts Shore.* Rinehart & Company, Inc., 1951

JOHNSON, AMANDUS *The Swedish Settlements on the Delaware.* 2v. University of Pennsylvania, 1911

MOURT, G. *A Relation, or Journall of the Beginnings and Proceedings of the English Plantation settled at Plimouth, in New England,* London, 1622

PERCY, GEORGE *An Account of Virginia.* London, 1608

SMITH, JOHN *A True Relation of Virginia.* London, 1608

INDEX

LOUISE DICKINSON RICH has long acquaintance with the early settlers. Growing up in Plymouth County, Massachusetts, in a family that came to the Old Bay Colony in its early days, she came to regard the Pilgrims as well-known friends, and developed a lasting interest in their way of living and that of settlers in other colonies. New England, where she still lives, has been the background for her many other books, among them *We Took to the Woods; The Peninsula; Innocence Under the Elms; The Coast of Maine; The Start of the Trail;* and *The First Book of New England.*

•

DOUGLAS GORSLINE is a graduate of the Art Students League, and in addition to having illustrated a variety of books by other authors, is author and illustrator of two of his own: *What People Wore* and *Farm Boy.* His work is represented in Pennsylvania Academy of Fine Arts, Corcoran Art Gallery, Chicago Art Institute, Whitney Museum of American Art, the National Academy of Design, and other art centers.